Poems from the Heart, Conversations with God is one man's walk with a loving God that began on January 6, 1987 and continues to this day.

Poems from the Heart, Conversations with God not only contains God's wonderful love in words, but also His love for us as shown through incredible images. Now all can say that they have seen God and the door to His kingdom with their own blessed eyes.

We all have a path in life that God has given us; may *Poems from the Heart, Conversations with God* be an inspiration during your own personal journey.

Poems From the Heart,

Conversations With God

James Michael DeStefano

First published by Dog Ear Publishing
4010 W. 86th Street, Ste H
Indianapolis, IN 46268
www.dogearpublishing.net

dog ear
PUBLISHING

ISBN: 1-59858-164-3
Library of Congress Control Number: 2006928004

This book is printed on acid-free paper.

Printed in the United States of America

Foreword

And the Lord said, "Come take my hand; love me, trust me, and walk with me down a path I have set forth for you. You will not walk this path alone, for I will always be there with you.

Look up with your eyes; my holiest of spirits will always be there for you to give you strength during your time of pain and sorrow.

Down this path you will walk through some of life's greatest pains and greatest losses, but because of your faith in me, you will be justly rewarded and blessed in every outcome.

I do this not only for you, but for all of my children, for if they believe in me like you do, they will never be left alone. I will always be there with them.

Know that through you they will find me, for your faith alone will save millions."

"Having been tested through suffering, He is able to help those who are tested..."
(Hebrews 2:18)

The Beginning of the Journey

And so, I would reach out to my Heavenly Father, and with my whole heart, soul, mind, and body, I would dedicate myself to Him and to all that He would ask of me on this special journey, for He is my Father and I am His son.

Poems from the Heart, Conversations with God was written as I walked with our Heavenly Father through some of life's greatest losses, such as: death, disease, divorce, disability, depression, and separation from my two wonderful children. During the most painful points of each loss, I would begin to communicate to our Heavenly Father through my writings, asking Him for the love, strength, guidance, and understanding necessary to make it through.

What I received back from our Heavenly Father was not only what I had asked for, but also a wonderful insight into His tremendous love for we, His children. The beautiful words and images he shared with me are now being shared with you in this wonderful book. These gifts are from a very loving Father who wants us to know that our faith and love in Him will get us through any of life's painful losses, as well as the physical, emotional, and spiritual pain associated with each one.

For each one of us who has ever had their faith challenged in the past, for those of us who may have had their faith challenged today, and for all of us who may have their faith challenged in the future, I am here as your personal witness, for I have walked the walk that our Heavenly Father has asked of me. In doing so, I have come through these losses as a better person, as a better Christian, and as a child of God, who today has an even deeper love and devotion for our Heavenly Father.

Are you ready to embark on your personal journey today? May God bless you and keep you in His care.

September 28, 1995

*****

To live
To love
To laugh
To cry
All are emotions
That we face till we die.

How we preclude
Our lives as a whole
Are the questions to answer
That come from our soul.

To die before death
Is a sin for all man
For to quit before death
Is the hourglass without sand.

How suddenly swift
We let grief overtake us
But being God's children
Know He'll never forsake us!

*****

September 29, 1995

*****

Sharing the courage
That we get from our souls
It's faith's finest hour
It's life's stories never told.

The discipline and love
That we need to grow
Are learned through life
As the seeds that we sow.

Weakness and sin
They come from the mind
They're the doubts that we cast
Like the sun that won't shine.

Listen to your heart
It's the soul of your being
For when touched by God's love
There's no finer human being.

*****

October 1, 1995

*****

Faith is love
When you don't have an answer
It's the purest of hearts
That can overtake disaster.

Faith in God
Is a lifetime of living
It starts in the soul
And with a heart that's forgiving.

Faith is trust
In something you believe in
It's the stories in the Bible
That give you a good feeling.

You know about Faith
For it's in your heart
And when you recognize its beauty
Your life will then start!

*****

October 1, 1995

*****

Casting aside
The despair in our hearts
With God as our ally
It's the place we must start.

Giving up hope
When the pain is so real
Is the greatest of tests
For the love we conceal.

To live for our Lord
Is to follow His laws
It's that hope in our lives
That we've never known before.

Today is the day
That your life takes on meaning
For in God there is hope
And a heart that has feeling.

*****

October 4, 1995

*****

Loving enough
To give of oneself
It's our sacrifice in life
That measures our worth.

When it seems hard to give
When your mind says no
Check with your heart
And the love in your soul.

There are people on Earth
Who sacrifice each day
They give out of love
They give what they may.

Living today
In a world full of greed
Takes a special kind of person
To help those in need.

So give what you can
Be it a prayer or a hand
Do it for the father
And be thankful that you can.

*****

October 17, 1995

*****

The test of time
Throughout the ages
Is our personal growth
Throughout life's stages.

The pain we feel
This very day
Is our personal test
Sent God's own way.

This may sound strange
For God is not pain
But it's in these tests
That we adhere to his reign.

Our God is love
His tests are just
He answers the prayers
Of those created from dust.

*****

October 19, 1995

*****

He's God's great Son
Who came here on Earth
A triumph for man
Was our loving Savior's birth.

His life was one of teaching
Each day He'd sacrifice
He asked His twelve to follow Him
That day would change their lives.

Many came from foreign lands
All had come to see
Was this our Savior Jesus
Who had come to set us free?

Those who had an earthly reign
Were threatened by His power
They plotted to destroy Him
But it became His finest hour.

Today He is in Heaven
At the right hand of the Father
Our goal in life must be His
Or his love can go no further.

*****

November 7, 1995

*****

Turning your life
Completely around
Is facing your pain
With your feet on the ground.

No one ever
Has to do it alone
For in Our Lord's own words
"Our path will be shown."

The work that is needed
To turn life around
Is prayer and fast
And a faith that is sound.

Our life's weaknesses
Our life's sins
They all must be confirmed
To be one with Him.

So cast away your doubts
And cast away your sorrows
For with God in your life
There's a wonderful tomorrow.

*****

December 11, 1995

*****

Sins of time
As we mature
We no longer see the truth
For we have become our own law.

Listening to love
Has it gone out the door?
Does the pain that we feel
Make each day a chore?

For the one who believes
Who looks sin in the eye
Takes a much greater strength
In order to survive.

Faith in believing
It's doing what feels right
It's listening to our heart
And not what's in sight.

Gaining true love
Admitting we are lost
Takes a great deal of courage
Sometimes at great costs.

Life goes so quickly
Isn't it time to take a stance?
Let's turn our lives to God
For it might be our last chance.

*****

December 11, 1995

*****

Discovering your life
What do you see?
Are you happy now?
Are you where you want to be?

Living and loving
Happiness and health
Are all important
Especially to oneself.

The key to oneself
The key to your life
It's not your children
Husband or wife.

Living with the Spirit
Knowing Him well
Is a key to a life
And a way out of Hell.

Look deep inside
What do you feel?
Is it your goodness of heart
Or your lies that you conceal?

So just for today
Be the best you can be
Do it with God
And He'll be there for thee!

*****

January 12, 1996

*****

The words are often different
Their sounds like none before
We say them in a special place
To the one that we adore.

A letter or a phrase
A question or a thought
The deeper meaning that we speak
Is often what is sought.

So, today give praise to our loving Lord
Give Him praise through your prayer
Let your praise come from your heart
And let Him know you care.

*****

March 14, 1996

*****

Questions and answers
Our ability to learn
But do we have the interest
Or do we let our souls burn?

Interest and trust
The opposite of power
The path to one's heart
Being discovered every hour.

Quality versus quantity
The best of behavior
The discovery in one's life
That we truly have a Savior.

The giving of one's life
The dedication of one's soul
The importance of spirituality
Must be our life's goal.

*****

March 15, 1996

*****

Pain is such a powerful word
The kind that makes one feel
There are so many levels
Each one so very real.

Pain affects one's attitude
Pain can change life's role
Pain can cause distractions
And pain can challenge one's soul.

When one reaches their limit
And exhausts all physical means
Physically and emotionally
Life's negativity can be seen.

But there is a wonderful alternative
That can take your pain away
It's the faith that lies within one's soul
It's the words we use to pray.

So, know today within your heart
When pain affects your day
That the Lord is there to help us all
If you would only begin to pray.

*****

March 24, 1996

*****

Loving someone
Giving it your all
Do you sometimes feel you give too much
Or not enough at all?

Lack of commitment
Lack of control
Does it make us want to quit
Or maybe give up our souls?

Our love must be
A two-hearted affair
For one without the other
Makes our loves so very unfair.

So in looking for love
Let it never overtake us
For our hearts may be forgiving
But our soul is for He who made us.

*****

April 2, 1996

*****

Life's inner child
It's a feeling that's so free
Within our hearts and within our souls
Is the person they call "me".

The fear and the pain
In this world in which we live
Are the sins committed by all mankind
In a world that won't forgive.

How are we to nurture
The love within our hearts
If each and every day we live
Our hearts are torn apart.

So let today be the day
That your healing does begin
Attach your heart to Jesus Christ
And you'll soon be free of sin.

*****

May 1, 1996

*****

His image and His likeness
His beauty so very true
His heart He opened to all mankind
But was accepted by so very few.

His eternal life and love
Have endured the test of time
The Bible, His eternal word
Each day our heavenly sign.

What more must He be
For He was given to thee
And as His word has endured
So has His love for me.

*****

May 24, 1996

*****

Like the sand upon one's sandals
Are the sins of all mankind
Many lost souls overwhelmed by sin
All looking for that one special sign.

In searching for help
What do we seek?
Shall we look to others
Or should I look inside me?

Life has many twists and turns
A sound foundation must be in place
But never has God ever turned His head
On a soul that was seeking His grace.

So set your sights on God's great law
And fill your heart with love
And as His love transcends upon you
Know it's the sign you asked for.

*****

June 26, 1996

*****

Happiness encircles
A heart full of love
And like the Heavens and the Earth
They're God's great love from above.

But so many souls are dejected
Unable to find their place
They look around all the wrong corners
Hoping to find God's grace.

To be led out of sin
Takes a soul in despair
Tired of hurting
In need of repair.

Tranquility and peace
They're God's gifts to us
But when taken for granted
They'll turn back into dust.

*****

July 1, 1996

*****

One day it happened
I don't know why
The physical pain
It made me cry.
My body now broken
Emotionally spent
I felt so alone
Not knowing where they went.

Lost completely
Body abused
No understanding
At why I was used.

Turning to God
He answered my prayer
For I cried from my heart
Putting my life in His care.

Today I am grateful
For I live His way
Not knowing about tomorrow
But living for today.

So thank you Lord
For rescuing me
My life is now yours
And my heart is for Thee.

*****

July 4, 1996

*****

A certain place
A certain time
A time in life
A time that's mine.

Searching inside
For the inner peace that's sought
Many challenges will be found
Many battles will be fought.

Our journey for peace
Is the reflection of our soul
Daily maintenance must be made
So that sin does not take control.

The love of God we have today
Must be paramount in our lives
For without our Lord's tremendous love
Our souls cannot survive.

*****

August 11, 1996

*****

To live life from the heart
Is to trust and be real
At times it may hurt
But true love is to feel.

To share your heart's message
Is to echo your dreams
It's allowing your love
To be shown and be seen.

Our loving inner child
So pure and so innocent
He's our lifeline to love
For all he's so significant.

Our loves and our spouses
Do they know what we share?
Do they know that our hearts
Are intertwined with theirs?

May this treasure called love
Found in the chest of our hearts
Bring happiness to our lives
Until the day we depart.

*****

September 26, 1996

*****

An amazing group together
They're the lifeline of those in need
They come together as Saint Vincent DePaul
They are God's most loving seeds.

A society based on the external
So many families lost
The heart of Saint Vincent DePaul
Is of our Lord and not of cost.

There are times in one's lifetime
When things may not go well
It's during these times in our lives
That we can call on Saint Vincent DePaul.

*****

September 26, 1996

*****

All the stars in the sky
With the planets and the sun
It can be the universe full of love
If it's God's will that will be done.

Amazing are the bodies
He created from space
More amazing is His love
His forgiveness, His grace.

Look at our bodies
An amazing piece of love
Constructed from dust
Designed by Him above.

If we dwell too deeply
On our creation as a whole
We will completely miss his message
That begins within our souls.

*****

October 1, 1996

*****

When tears and fears
Filled my life
It was the pain I felt
That was Satan's delight.

It was a time for me
To either live or die
For my heart was broken
And my eyes did cry.

But deep down inside
We are born with control
It's God's greatest gift
It's His gift of our soul.

The soul is our foundation
It's our connection with the Lord
It teaches us to live
With love and not the sword.

To turn to God
When you are down
Takes a certain kind of strength
A gift that's so profound.

But you need not wait
For pain to arrive
For with God in your life
You are truly alive.

*****

October 7, 1996

*****

The peaceful existence
That comes from within
Is the voice of our Lord
Saying, "Choose love over sin."

Loneliness can be a forgiving place
It's alone with oneself
That lets us search for His grace.

Spiritual weakness
Will cause us sin
These are the troubles
That hurt from within.

A glorious path
That we can follow
Starts from the heart
Even in sorrow.

To find love in pain
Is hope with no ending
It's a grace from the soul
That our Lord keeps on sending.

*****

October 9, 1996

*****

God's miracle is love
It happens every day
It's the little things that happen
That tell us it's okay.

Big miracles
Small miracles
Miracles in all sizes
A miracle from God
Comes from love and not surprises.

Being in tune
To all of life's greetings
It's the spiritual side of life
That many of us are deleting.

A miracle will happen
When your heart is with the Father
For it's on this road of life
That His miracles let us go farther.

*****

October 9, 1996

*****

Lest we forget
This land that we live
This great planet Earth
That our Holy Father hath give.

The rivers and streams
This land He hath dreamed
So to give it it's birth
He created this Earth.

This land and its riches
This land of plenty
But it's pollution and destruction
Are being done by so many.

The hope that we hold
Is in our children's hearts
For it is we their parents
Who must now do our part.

To Our Father in Heaven
There are no words to say
For the greed that brings destruction
Must not last another day.

*****

October 10, 1996

*****

To be free from despair
Takes truth over dare
For the pain that we feel
Can be our fate that is sealed.

The destruction of life
It fills all emotions
It's the opposite of birth
That puts our lives in motion.

We were born pure
It's life that is pain
For in loving the sun
We must deal with the rain.

Giving up
Seeing no end
It's this time in our life
That the spirit will descend.

Some of these tests
Why are they a must
It's the pain that we feel
That always shakes our trust.

But it must be God's plan
It must show that He cares
For He comes with His love
To take away our despair.

*****

October 24, 1996

*****

Living and learning
They go hand in hand
They are both tied together
Like the emotions of man.

Letting your gift
Be discarded as waste
Is a sin for the soul
For which life is based.

Calling to God
For His strength and His pardon
Means finding oneself
Like the Agony in the Garden.

To resurrect your gift
Means checking your soul
It's our own inner fight
That lets us be whole.

Listen to your heart
For it beats for the Father
It's this language called love
That lets us try harder.

*****

December 5, 1996

*****

Our triumphs in life
To some may be strange
But what is of importance
Is our willingness to change.

Love like a fire
Can shine so brightly
But without God's love
It can only grow slightly.

Change is a word
That we fear so much
During life comes change
May it be with God's touch.

Let go and let God
It's easier said than done
But in listening to the Spirit
Do we follow God's son?

So just for today
Be the best you can be
Let God's love overcome you
So your life will be free.

*****

December 12, 1996

*****

Lending to life
His emotional joy
These feelings of warmth
Brought by God's little boy.

His family of love
Overcame most
Guided by the Spirit
That joins in the Host.

Worldly treasure
Of worth such a few
The importance of God
Is His eternal love for you.

The truest of loves
The wealth of the soul
There is no love that is finer
When His life is our goal.

*****

December 23, 1996

*****

The beat of our hearts
The breaths that we take
All gifts from the Lord
That we should never forsake.

All through our day
Do we ever take the time
To look towards the Heavens
And thank God we are fine?

It may come in an instant
It may come in a flash
Our life as we know it
Can end with a crash.

Let this day of your life
Be the best it can be
Thank God for your life
And offer it to He.

*****

December 24, 1996

*****

Do you measure your worth
By the money you make
The jewelry you wear
The people you forsake?

Or has your life this day
Found its true worth
By the heart that you have
And the love of His birth?

The truly rich of this world
Are rich in His spirit
They live for His love
And there is no day they must fear it.

To have true worth
Is to acknowledge Him above
It's a soul full of faith
And a heart full of love.

*****

December 24, 1996

*****

Humble of heart
Humble of mind
Opened to the Spirit
One day at a time.

This life is our gift
So precious to me
Never take it for granted
For it can be taken from thee.

Change is not easy
In life as we grow
For to live for the Lord
Means to never say no.

I have been humbled
My life has changed
For He heard my cries
As I walked in pain.

With God in my life
Today I can see
For in receiving His Son
He also saved me.

*****

December 26, 1996

*****

Alone with a mood
A presence so bare
In the evening it's frightening
During the light it's despair.

Isolated feelings
Turning like the sun
One minute freedom
The next minute none.

How can we live
How will we die
How can we begin
With fear in our eyes?

Turn your hearts to love
Let your moods follow
What is life without God
But only empty and hollow?

*****

December 28, 1996

*****

Life's greatest pleasure
Is the true love in one's heart
It's a feeling that is special
But it's our decision when to start.

Many of us can't agree
What to others is so clear
It's our ability to believe
And our faith overcoming our fears.

Our lifeline to this special love
Is the peace by which we live
Even in feeling life's great pain
We must be willing to forgive.

The guidelines to a life of love
Remains steadfast throughout the ages
It's in following the laws of Our Lord
And letting Him cleanse our rages.

Today can be your start anew
Your first day of true love
Start by being true to you
And the rest will be sent from above.

*****

December 30, 1996

*****

Living, loving, beginning to grow
The basic life essentials
If it's God's love we're to know.

The love we choose
The lives we embrace
All are the gifts
That make up His grace.

The Sacraments
The Mass
Our spiritual health
Gifts that fulfill
They're our eternal wealth.

Lacking in knowledge
An excuse, not a flaw
Know of His Commandments
For they are His loving laws.

And as our lives unfold
And our stories are told
If we have lived for Our Lord
Then our lives were like gold.

*****

January 3, 1997

*****

A world full of fears
How are we to trust?
Do we give into Satan
Or the one who is just?

From childhood to adulthood
From shore to shore
We are all God's children
In this we can be sure.

It's there for us to choose
But it's also there to lose
So let the decision that we make
Never ever be confused.

Choosing God is choosing good
It's being on the winning team
So let your hearts be full of love
And your God will fulfill your dreams.

*****

The Pictures

The pictures on the following pages are the first pictures ever given to mankind that allow us to actually see our Heavenly Father, His Holy Trinity, and the actual door to His Kingdom in Heaven with our own eyes while we were still alive.

I have had these pictures since 1992, four years after my journey with our Heavenly Father began, and I was asked to walk a path with Him, so that He could help all mankind even more than He already has.

Imagine taking pictures of what you perceive as a "spinning sun" with nothing else in the sky, and receiving pictures of our Heavenly Father, His Most Holy Trinity, and two beautiful pictures of "the door to Heaven." I can only describe my initial reactions as those that ran the gambit from gratitude to disbelief, from love to extreme happiness.

In the next few pages of this book, I am about to share with you pictures that our Heavenly Father has shared with me since that special day in 1992.

The reasons we have been given these pictures is because our Heavenly Father wants us to have no doubt that He and His Most Holy Trinity are all very, very real.

The writings in this book were also given to us by our Heavenly Father. As I experienced some of the greatest losses in life, He would give me the words and love from His own heart, to know that with Him we can endure all things, and overcome any of life's losses.

What a tremendously loving Father, a Father that loves us all, a Father that wants all of us to be His loving children.

I have been asked to publish this book at this time by our Heavenly Father, and I pray that it will give you the personal relationship and strength to stay true to Him as it has for me.

May God always bless you and his family and keep you all in his care,

Jim

When I took the picture that you will see on the next page, and the pages that follow, only the sun that I perceived as spinning in the sky was present for me to see.

What I received after the picture was taken was the picture of a beautiful doorway in the middle of the sky. It was a picture of "The Entrance to Our Heavenly Father's Kingdom of Heaven."

As you look at this picture, you can also see a cross in the middle of the door, with what looks to be the fire of the most Holy Spirit right in the middle, as if holding the cross together.

On the bottom of the picture there appears to be a face, possibly made out of stone, but a face nevertheless that looks in a great deal of pain, quite possibly because it will never enter into God's Kingdom.

Remember God's Commandments were given to us for a reason, and this reason was to allow all of us entrance into our Heavenly Father's Kingdom of Heaven and eternal life.

P67—The Door to Heaven

This picture is exactly like the first one except for two differences. The first difference is that it was taken on the other side of the world in Medjugorje in the old country, Yugoslavia, and the cloud entering the picture from the left that is signifying the cloud of doubt.

This cloud will always block us from the light of God if we do not believe in our Heavenly Father with childlike faith and love.

If I doubted that I was seeing a spinning sun in the sky, I too would have been blocked from this beautiful picture from God. We must all believe like the children we are.

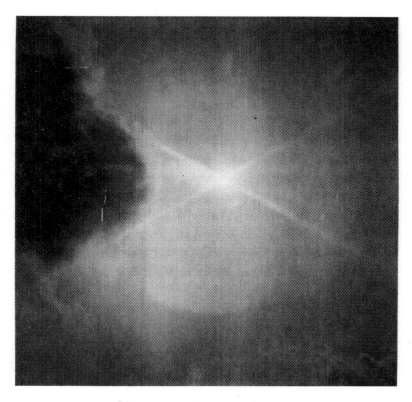

P69—The Door to Heaven

This is the first pictures ever taken of our Heavenly Father Himself, but He did not come alone for He allows us to see Him as three, as in His most "Holy Trinity."

As you look at the picture, in the upper right hand corner, you can see his face with white hair and a white beard. His face is inside the outline (three-quarters) of our Savior's cross with the fire of the most Holy Trinity in the middle. What a gift from our loving Father.

P71—The Most Holy Trinity

Since 1992, I have been allowed to see this vision of our Heavenly Father's Most Holy Spirit on a daily basis. It is quite possibly the greatest gift I have ever been granted, and today I share it with you in picture form.

The circle of white has lights that the small heavenly body attaches itself to, and then in a circular motion, always appears to be circling in a way that takes it straight up in the sky until it disappears.

Thank you, Heavenly Father.

P73—The Holy Spirit

This picture is difficult to see because it is a small profile picture of our Lord's Mother, "The Blessed Virgin Mary." As she looks up to the light of God, you can notice Her crown, with a small picture of her eyes, nose, and chin to follow.

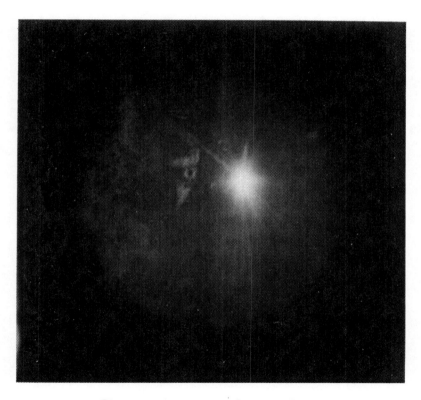

P75—The Blessed Virgin Mary

I shared this picture with a friend who happens to be in the clergy. He showed me that this picture has the display of a father followed by a mother, standing on a cloud, with their little child behind them, lying on the cloud. In essence, it is a picture of the family, looking up to the light of the Lord.

I believe our Heavenly Father is sharing with us the importance of family to Him, and how we, his children, must make a better effort to preserve the family unit today in our society.

P77—The Family

We all know the greatness of our late Pontiff. In this picture, you can see his red hat, with his face and shoulders. Around his shoulders, you can see his rosary and at the end of the rosary, in the middle of his chest, you can see the crucifix.

If you have trouble making out some of the more difficult pictures, please take a minute to say a prayer, and ask God for help.

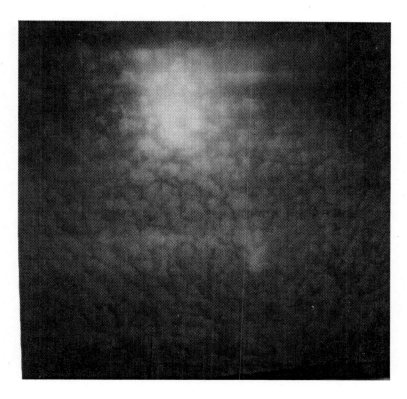

P79—Pope John Paul II

I had this picture for three years before I heard a voice saying, "Turn the picture upside down." There, on the lower right, you can see his two eyes, nose, mustache, goatee, and even horns coming out of his head. He is true evil and truly real.

P81—Satan

January 27, 1997

*****

Lost hopes
Lost dreams
Tears from the eyes
Is it really what it seems?

Crushed and depressed
Feelings lost
Never give up
No matter the cost.

My faith, my love
My Father above
Please free me this day
From these feelings with love.

All is never lost
When it's the Father you're in tune
For He says through our loving hearts
That our dreams will truly come soon.

*****

January 28, 1997

*****

Thwarted with rejection
The feelings of pain
Keeping up hope
Sometimes mundane.

Seeing and feeling
Loving and prayer
Life's greatest assets
Discarding we don't dare.

Life's lonesome highway
Never quite feeling right
Soon it will happen
For with God it's always in sight.

So today let go
Let today feel right
Let this day be special
As you follow God's shining light.

*****

February 10, 1997

*****

Be open to the Spirit
Please don't ever be afraid
Fear is in our running
When we know we should have stayed.

The love of His tender touch
It transcends through us all
But it cannot come within us
If we put up our defensive walls.

The Father and the Son
With the love of the Spirit
It's a gift to us all
But so many of us fear it.

It is so hard
To do what is right
Is it easier in the darkness?
Or is it better in the light?

We must open our hearts
In time to be healed
For within our acceptance
His great love is concealed.

*****

February 15, 1997

*****

Prayer is a gift
Never take it for granted
For the prayers that you say
Are the seeds that are planted.

Pity on those
Who cannot pray
Many do try
But many more say nay.

A life of self
Neglecting prayer
The self is their limit
For no others can they care.

A balance and union
To one's Higher Power
Is a gift and a must
That cannot wait one more hour.

So give your heart to God
For it's in the beauty of your prayer
It shows that you love Him
It shows how much you care.

*****

February 17, 1997

*****

Longing for happiness
It starts with the truth
It's the man in the mirror
And what you want to do.

Do you give it all up
At the drop of a dime
Or is it worth all of your prayers
And all of your time?

Our lives have stages
Each one lets us grow
It's not what you've seen
But it's in God's word you must know.

May true happiness be yours
May your life have peace
May you align your hearts with God's
And your troubles will forever cease.

*****

February 21, 1997

*****

With childlike confidence
I come to thee
Willing to let go
And willing to be me.

To trust in His Son
Is not easily done
For with life's worldly pleasures
We are detached from His Son.

No matter your age
No matter your race
It can only start with you
When you say yes to His grace.

Before you continue
Your life on this earth
Give it all to the Father
Who knows your true worth.

*****

March 8, 1997

*****

To walk down the path
The path that leads home
Takes a lifetime of steps
Some seen, some unknown.

The path of life
With its hills and curves
Is walked by all
But to some is self-served.

Every step is crucial
Every step points the way
Every step takes longer
For those who say nay.

But for those who travel
Within His great light
There is a lifetime of love
And a path that is right.

*****

March 13, 1997

*****

Trying this day
To overcome sin
Do we know of the tools
That are available from Him?

Everything is there
It's been written through time
It's up to us to want it
For so long we've been blind.

In opening your heart
You open your soul
You're asking for help
You're doing what's told.

In God there is love
That overcomes all
It's a power and strength
That's awaiting your call.

*****

March 21, 1997

*****

Love so splendid
Love so dear
Love with your heart
And never love in fear.

Waiting and watching
To talk and to listen
This phase is so painful
But I must trust if I am Christian.

So blessed be you My Lord
May your blessings see us through
For you give us your love, Oh Lord
And a happiness that's true.

*****

April 9, 1997

*****

To dream is a passage
A voyage to new heights
A dream can be fulfilling
If we keep our goals in sight.

Some of us dream of money
Others dream of love
But some of us are unable to dream
So we pray to God above.

Many dreams can bring us pain
Sometimes too hard for thought
It is these painful dreams of night
That awake are never sought.

Let your dreams be full of happiness
Let your dreams be filled with love
Let your dreams you have today
Be inspired by God above.

*****

April 28, 1997

*****

Hollow is the heart
That loves on a whim
Shallow is the love
When it's wed in sin.

Diligent is the mind
When used to explore
But fostered are the emotions
That are not of the core.

Try as you may
Try as you might
If it's not true to oneself
Then what good is the fight?

*****

May 1, 1997

*****

In loneliness and loss
Many hearts are broken
The repair seems endless
Your memories but a token.

For love to end
Means a blow to your heart
It's an unwanted feeling
One you wish would depart.

Life has its stages
And from beginning to end
Each stage has its feelings
Each stage has its end.

In life as in love
We must learn how to live
Always looking to grow
Always looking to give.

Know in your heart
That when you love another
It was a gift from the Lord
And also His Mother.

*****

May 1, 1997

*****

The heart of a child
So virgin so pure
This heart new to life
Too young to know more.

Each day of its life
This heart will endure
Many of life's problems
In its fight to stay pure.

Our society is in turmoil
We kill and start wars
Our children are our future
Their hearts are our core.

Each day Our Lord grants us
The tools that we need
Beautiful new children
Our society's new seeds.

For our society to heal
We must love and must trust
For God works through His children
Who grow up to be us.

*****

May 5, 1997

*****

Tools for Loving God

Daily prayer
Weekly fast
Living the Commandments
Going to mass.

If we put these gifts in motion
We as Christians will fulfill
The laws that He has written
The ones for which He willed.

So I thank you, Lord
This day with prayer
For each day is a gift
In which I can show I care.

*****

May 9, 1997

*****

The strength to endure
The faith to keep growing
I love you my Lord
But my trust is not showing.

It's those days that I feel
That there is nothing to learn
That the road in my life
Starts to twist and to turn.

So let us continue
Through all of life's stages
To accept Our Lord's love
That has been passed throughout the ages.

*****

June 3, 1997

*****

In life's great plan
We will have good and bad
Happiness and health
And disappointments that are sad.

Our life's greatest virtue
Is one that's a must
It's our love for God
In whom we must trust.

Our monetary treasures
Our anger and descent
They all offend the laws
That our Mighty Lord has sent.

Strength from love
It's found in our prayers
It's God's great gift
And shows how much He cares.

*****

June 17, 1997

*****

With maximum love
I follow my Lord
But the complexities of life
Must never sever the cord.

To live in this world
Brings many distractions
Each pulling us away
From our most important attraction.

Balance in life
Is what keeps us sane
But love for our Lord
Is what we must maintain.

So live this life
The one He has given
But keep Him first
And for your faith, be driven.

*****

August 1, 1997

*****

He came to me one special day
He would show Himself this way
My heart was full of pain that day
It was lost and full of dismay.

The praise and prayers that came from my heart
Were the seeds of our relationship right from the start
Many days I know I let Him down
He knows my weakness, I can see him frown.

The love and trust He has in me
Have opened my heart and set me free
One thing is certain this very day
He is my God, a friend today.

*****

August 3, 1997

*****

Harboring fears
That steal our emotions
It's a lifetime of longing
Like lost ships in the ocean.

How are we able
To grow in the Spirit
When we are the ones
Who constantly fear it?

Going through life
Afraid of mistakes
When we never give a thought
To the One we forsake.

Lost in fear
Distraught and dismayed
It's two steps back
In this world in which we stay.

We were not created
To live our lives in fear
But rather we were born
For to Him we are dear.

*****

October 8, 1997

*****

To be oneself
To live for today
It's a gift to oneself
Sent the Lord's way.

To love and be friendly
To help and to save
Without looking for applause
It's a gift that God gave.

Each day we have choices
To smile or be sad
In a world full of pain
Let God be your dad.

I know in my heart
That I live with much pain
But with God in my life
There's no reason to complain.

*****

October 8, 1997

*****

Disappointed and discouraged
Abandoned and alone
Physically and emotionally
Those around me turned to stone.

My heart is beating loudly
It's never known such pain
Those that had surrounded me
Said my message was in vain.

I've never known such loss, Oh Lord
My family is not true
All I ever did, Oh Lord
Was show them my love for you.

I still ask you for a miracle, Lord
For I know you love them too
Please bring my family home, Oh Lord
So we can live our lives with you.

*****

November 3, 1997

*****

Renewed in the Spirit
Blessed by God above
A new day beginning
Let this day be blessed in love.

With all of life's problems
And with all of life's pain
I ask my Lord's protection
So that my love is not in vain.

I cannot have love
I cannot have peace
I cannot begin to live
Until my sins have ceased.

Today I renew my birth
My connection with God above
For today I am a Christian
One that knows how to truly love.

*****

January 3, 1998

*****

To the Father:

I share my heart
With you this day
My soul, our connection
It is to you that I pray.

This love I feel
This love I share
It's my loving commitment
To He whom I care.

I've learned so much
From a heart that was broken
So this love for you
From my heart it is spoken.

This truest of loves
That I have for Thee
Is reinforced each day
As I pray from my knee.

*****

January 11, 1998

*****

To grow with our Lord
Is from day to day
With love from the heart
And our willingness to pray.

Neither man nor woman
Upon this earth
Would be able to grow
If not for His birth.

But some of us
Are empty inside
While others are lost
And just want to cry.

So how are we
To grow this day
If our hearts are closed
And we've lost our way?

But our loving Lord has promised
If our work will soon begin
That He our great and mighty Lord
Would free us from our sins.

So now my life has meaning
As I pray each beautiful day
Today I have a chance to grow
If I live my life His way.

*****

January 15, 1998

*****

The winds and the clouds
The sun and the rain
All set to a picture
All are God's terrain.

But to live in the today
And love the right way
Means to turn to the Spirit
And to follow His way.

To be willing to be taught
In the proper light
Means to listen to the Spirit
And to obey what is right.

What transpires on Earth
For us in a day
Will come to an end
Quite suddenly one day.

But your life will never end
For I know this to be true
If you have faith in the Spirit
He will always be there for you.

*****

February 10, 1998

*****

Each day we must try
To follow His law
To receive the Sacraments
That lead to Heaven's Door.

His Mother has come
To lead us Home
She asks us to pray
To fast and to atone.

Do we understand the gifts
That Our Father has sent:
His Son, Our Lady,
The Spirit's descent?

Do we do to His Mother
What they did to Him
Do we believe in His Mother
Who leads us from sin?

The steps of your life
Are precious and few
Live them for God
And He will forever love you.

*****

March 19, 1998

*****

Staggered by pain
Surrounded by loss
Holding on to God
No matter the cost.

Hurting so bad
Feeling so low
Holding on tight
To a love that I know.

Enemies surround me
They make themselves known
They thirst for my termination
For they think I am alone.

But my God of love
Will never leave me alone
For He knows in my heart
How my faith has grown.

*****

March 30, 1998

*****

Never judge another
Like a book's outer cover
For in being God's children
We must love one another.

The beauty that be
Must be fulfilled within me
For in helping God's children
We must be true to He.

So in going through life
Try to understand what is right
For the heart of a child
Will always shine with God's light.

*****

May 2, 1998

*****

Trust is accepting who we are
It's that beautiful inner feeling
That helps us go far.

Lasting relationships
With communication and trust
Can open up hearts
To those who are just.

The family is a structure
That can work very well
It takes two to make it
Or to let it get dull.

Love from your heart
For it is God's special gift
And when two people can trust
Their love will not drift.

*****

May 12, 1998

*****

Lying awake
When I should be asleep
Fears fill my mind
My anxiety so deep.

Thoughts of resolution
Sprinkled in with grief
My heart beats quickly
As my mind seeks relief.

But warmth fills my heart
As my mind finds its role
My thoughts turn to Jesus
And the love within my soul.

In one loving moment
My anxiety subsides
For in turning to the Father
My fear can no longer hide.

*****

May 12, 1998

*****

What is true love
Where is it found
Do you look from within
Or do you look to the ground?

To many of us
Love is unknown
Growing up in a family
Without love being shown.

The trauma that results
Is the fear of the unknown
For two people to love
Connected hearts must have grown.

Many today
They walk around lost
They think of the ways
To find love at all costs.

But love can be simple
And love can be true
For if today you love Jesus
True love will fill you.

*****

September 12, 1998

*****

I lie awake
Heart beating fast
Alone with myself
How long will this last?

Tired and helpless
My heart so blue
My God, my Lord
My prayers so true.

Today in our world
So much pain and sin
Hearts so cold
Souls like tin.

My Lord I pray
Please awaken these sinners
For all of your children
Were born to be winners.

*****

December 21, 1998

*****

Oh, true lover of souls
Oh, true lover of all men
Deliver my soul from the depths of despair
Deliver my soul from the damned.

Oh, eternal love
Please guide my path this day
For my sins are many
But your love shows me the way.

Forgiving Father of Love
Today you've rescued me
And so I offer you my being
For your forgiveness has set me free.

The heart and soul within us
They're a special gift and grace
And if they evolve the way God asks
In Heaven we will find our place.

*****

January 1, 1999

*****

The Sacrament of marriage
A blessing from the Lord
But today within society
Divorce severs the cord.

Harmony and trust
To be loyal and in love
Bliss is never day-to-day
Like a snow white virgin dove.

Believing in love
Believing in each other
Takes two hearts filled with faith
Like Saint Joseph and God's Holy Mother.

When times get tough
When your love begins to dim
Look up to Heaven
And remember your love for him.

*****

February 22, 1999

*****

Resilience for me
Is to have faith in He
For the evil that men do
Will not destroy me.

What is this faith
From where is its strength
How does one begin
To attain it at length?

Faith is love
And a belief that's unending
It's on days filled with rain
That faith's love is so defending.

In this world filled with pain
In this world filled with sin
Your faith in God
Is your ticket to win.

*****

January 18, 2002

*****

The gift that He gave
Is the love in your heart
It shines in your smile
It's been there from the start.

Working with children
God's special joy
You gave of yourself
To God's little boy.

But success turns to failure
When consumed by one
For many times unknowingly
We delete God's son.

But winning in life
Is learning to believe
For these young children
Are God's faithful new seeds.

So remember this day
That God gave you this chance
For it's the hearts of these children
That you were asked to enhance.

*****

December 7, 2002

*****

One hundred percent
Father, how do I do it
For my commitment to you
Is never to lose it.

Bad days, good days
Days of sun and rain
But a day without you, Lord
Is a day filled with pain.

Lord, my heart is yours
My love is real
Help me Heavenly Father
So this day I may heal.

*****

January 10, 2003

*****

Hollow the heart
And empty the soul
When loving from the heart
Is not your life's goal.

It's in cherishing this emotion
That our lives can unfold
For the love in our heart
Is worth more than pure gold.

So go forth this day
And let love be your core
For this gift from the Father
Is the key to Heaven's Door.

*****

January 17, 2003

*****

Let God's great love
Overwhelm your heart
So that your love of Him
Will never depart.

Our lives are priceless
When we live for Him
For He is our Savior
Who overcame sin.

His life our goal
His will our soul
Without his love
It's a death we will know.

So be it today
Or be it tomorrow
In choosing God's love
You may finally release your sorrow.

*****

January 17, 2003

*****

They're numbered to ten
Since creation they've been
But when in your life
Have you lived up to them?

Suffice it to say
That they all are not easy
But to live life without them
Is a choice that's too easy.

So say as you may
And say as you might
It's these great ten
That keep Heaven in sight.

*****

January 18, 2003

*****

This rage we feel
This pain so true
Known by many
Overcome by few.

In the darkest of hours
When the light is unseen
We feel lost in a world
Thinking like a dream.

To dismiss this time
As the pain unfolds
Takes the strongest of faiths
And a heart that's not cold.

In searching for the answer
Pray from your knees
For all prayers are answered
And in God's time you will see.

So go forth this day
And walk through your pain
For the God whom you love
Will never let you suffer in vain.

*****

Epilogue

February 9, 2003

To be able to witness for God's children is the greatest gift that anyone could be given in their lifetime. I am so very grateful to God for using me as an instrument of His peace. However, all that I have been through will mean nothing, if you my brothers and sisters in Christ do not begin your own personal journey with our Lord today.

I pray that the poems, conversations, and pictures within this book will inspire you to fulfill your own personal journey on Earth in the name of our Lord and Savior, Jesus Christ.

"The Spirit reveals His presence in each one with a gift, which is also a service..."
(Corinthians 12:7)

May God's love and peace be with you.

Love,
Jim

Printed in the United States
200174BV00002B/139-231/A

9 781598 581645